Animals That Store Food

Written by Kerrie Shanahan

Flying Start
to Literacy®

Contents

Introduction

Some animals that eat plants collect and store food so they have something to eat when they cannot find fresh food.

They collect the plants when they are available and store them to eat later.

Chapter 1

Storing seeds and nuts

Some animals collect and store seeds and nuts to eat. Seeds and nuts can be stored for a long time. They provide food for the animals during winter.

Acorn woodpeckers

Acorn woodpeckers collect and store acorns during summer and autumn.

They use their strong beaks to peck holes in dead tree trunks or wooden fence posts and they put one acorn in each hole. The holes are just the right size for an acorn to fit in tightly so that other animals cannot steal them.

When the stored acorns dry out, they shrink and become loose in their holes. The acorn woodpeckers then move them to new holes where they fit tightly and cannot be stolen.

Acorn woodpeckers eat the stored acorns in winter, when there isn't much other food.

Squirrels

Squirrels gather nuts and seeds which they bury in different places under the ground. This buried food is what the squirrels eat when they don't have fresh food to eat. Squirrels use their sense of smell to find the nuts and seeds they have buried.

Squirrels also store other foods, such as mushrooms, in the hollows of trees.

Squirrels have to look after their acorns so they will not go rotten.

Sometimes a worm burrows into an acorn that a squirrel has buried.
The worm can make the acorn rotten.
The squirrel will find this rotten acorn and throw it out before the rot spreads to all the other buried acorns.

If the acorns grow when they are buried, they are not good for the squirrels to eat.
So before the squirrels bury the acorns, they chew off the parts that might grow.

Chapter 2

Storing plants, leaves and bark

Some animals store plants, and parts of plants such as leaves and bark. They eat this food when there is no fresh food to eat.

Beavers

Beavers collect small trees which they store in an underwater dam. They trim off the branches with their teeth and drag the trees to their dam. The beavers eat the bark and the soft wood of the trees. Beavers eat other plants which they also store under water.

beaver dam

Pikas

Pikas eat grass. In summer and early autumn, pikas collect grass. They put the grass in piles in the sun so it dries out and turns to hay. Pikas turn the grass over often so that it dries faster.

When the grass has turned into hay, pikas store it in their burrow.

In winter, when the ground is covered in snow, pikas eat the hay they have stored inside their burrow.

Chapter 3

Storing nectar

Some animals
collect nectar from
flowers and store it.

Honeypot ants

Honeypot ants live in nests. There are two
different types of honeypot ants – worker
honeypot ants and storage honeypot ants.
They have different jobs to do in the nest.

Worker honeypot ants go out of the nest to
collect nectar from flowers. They swallow
the nectar then feed it to the storage
honeypot ants.

The storage honeypot ants store the nectar
in their stomachs.   The more nectar
they store, the bigger their stomachs get.
Their stomachs look like pots of honey.

When there is no fresh nectar, the
storage ants feed the nectar they
have stored to other ants in the nest.

Bees

Bees collect nectar from flowers. Bees can change the nectar into honey. When the nectar has been changed into honey, the bees empty it into honeycomb. The honey is stored there until the bees need it for food.

honey

bee

honeycomb

21

Conclusion

Some animals need to store food because fresh food is sometimes hard to find.

Animals that store food have clever ways of collecting and storing the food they need.

When animals have plenty of food stored they can survive the winter more easily.

Glossary

burrow   a hole in the ground usually made by an animal

bury   to put something under the ground

hollow   a space that is empty

honey pot   a container for storing honey

nectar   the sweet liquid from a plant

survive   to stay alive